PREHISTORIC BEASTS
OF THE
ICE AGE

TED RECHLIN

DOVER PUBLICATIONS, INC.
MINEOLA, NEW YORK

This fun and informative coloring book contains 44 illustrations showcasing the diverse animal life of the Pleistocene Epoch, better known as the Ice Age. Kids will have fun coloring the cave bear, woolly mammoth, and Irish elk, as well as giant birds and the sabertooth salmon. Plus, informative captions give a brief description of each Ice Age beast!

Bibliographical Note
Prehistoric Beasts of the Ice Age is a new work, first published by
Dover Publications, Inc., in 2016.

International Standard Book Number
ISBN-13: 978-0-486-80313-5
ISBN-10: 0-486-80313-9

Manufactured in the United States by LSC Communications
80313902   2017
www.doverpublications.com

AMERICAN CHEETAH

This fleet-footed predator lived on the plains of western North America. The cat used its incredible speed to chase down animals like the Pronghorn Antelope, a creature that outlived the American Cheetah and is still around today.

AMERICAN HYENA

The American Hyena, also called the Running Hyena, shared more physical characteristics with wolves and dogs than with most other hyena species. This Hyena's closest relative, the Aardwolf, is still alive today.

AMERICAN LION

The biggest big cat to have ever lived, the American Lion could grow to a size of more than 800 pounds. Unlike their modern relatives, male American Lions did not have manes.

AUROCHS

Weighing in at over 3,000 pounds, the Aurochs was one of the largest Bovine species ever. The Pleistocene beast did not go extinct until the year 1627. Its eventual demise was caused by a combination of overhunting, human development, and diseases spread by domestic cattle.

BONE-CRUSHING DOG

This carnivore was about the size of a modern coyote, but was much more powerfully built. It used its strong jaws to do just what its name suggests, crush bone. The Bone-Crushing Dog went extinct at the beginning of the Pleistocene Epoch, being superceded by more advanced canines.

CAVE BEAR

Similar in appearance to the modern Grizzly Bear, the Cave Bear could weigh as much as 1,200 pounds. Unlike other bear species that eat both meat and vegetation, the Cave Bear ate only plants. The bear gets its name because many skeletons of the species have been found in caves in Europe.

CAVE HYENA

Much larger than modern hyenas, the Cave Hyena was a predator that fed on large animals like horses and bison. The Cave Hyena was a rival of early humans, competing with them both for prey and the caves they liked to live in.

CHALICOTHERE

Chalicotheres were around for millions of years. The last species, Ancylotherium, lived into the early Pleistocene. This odd-looking beast was about the size of a large horse and fed on plants.

COLUMBIAN MAMMOTH

At more than 13 feet tall and 10 tons, the Columbian Mammoth was one of the largest elephants to have ever lived. Bigger even than the more famous Woolly Mammoth, the Columbian Mammoth lived in warmer climates and may not have been as furry as its woolly cousin.

CUBAN GIANT OWL

Around 4 feet tall, this was the largest owl to have ever lived. The Cuban Giant Owl was probably mostly flightless, climbing high into trees and then dropping down on unsuspecting prey such as large rodents and young ground sloths, killing them with its large foot talons.

DEINOTHERIUM

This giant species of elephant lived in Pleistocene Africa. It is easily recognized by its strange, downward-pointing tusks. It is possible that Deinotherium used these odd tusks for digging or to strip branches from trees.

DIPROTODON

Diprotodon was the largest marsupial to have ever lived. Its closest living relatives are tiny wombats, but this Australian mega-beast grew to be the size of a hippo.

DIRE WOLF

In appearance, the Dire Wolf looks very similar to its living cousin, the Gray Wolf. The Dire Wolf was slower than the Gray Wolf, but was stronger and hunted larger prey. When the giant herbivores of the Ice Age died out, the Dire Wolf was not fast enough to hunt the surviving prey species, leaving an opening for the Gray Wolf to become the dominant canine in North America.

DOEDICURUS

Doedicurus, like its modern relative the armadillo, was covered head to tail in thick armor. The only difference is that Doedicurus was a 4,000 pound armadillo, growing to the size of a small car.

ELASMOTHERIUM

Elasmotherium was one big rhino, growing as large as a mammoth. Looking more like a mythical unicorn than a rhino, Elasmortherium had one massive horn on its head and may have carried it upright like a horse.

ELEPHANT BIRD

The Elephant Bird grew to a gargantuan 10 feet tall and up to 1,000 pounds. Its twenty-pound eggs were the largest of any bird that has ever lived.

GIANT BEAVER

At 7 feet long and more than 250 pounds, the Giant Beaver was the largest rodent alive in North America during the Ice Age. While much bigger than its living relative, the Giant Beaver had a much smaller brain and is thought to have been considerably less intelligent than modern beavers.

GIANT CONDOR

With a 16 foot wingspan, this was the largest flying bird ever in North America. Though called a condor, this bird was similar to modern condors in appearance only and is actually a different species.

GIANT ECHIDNA

The Giant Echidna lived in Pleistocene Australia and was the largest monotreme, or egg-laying mammal, to have ever lived. It used its long snout and tongue to feed on insects. This strange creature's smaller, egg-laying cousins still live on today.

GIANT LEMUR

The Giant Lemur grew to the size of a Silverback Gorilla. It was one of the largest primates to have ever existed, and was the largest to have ever inhabited the island of Madagascar.

GIANT SHORT-FACED BEAR

Unlike most other bears, the Giant Short-Faced Bear was exclusively carnivorous, eating only meat. At 13 feet tall and more than 2,500 pounds, the Giant Short-Faced bear was the largest mammalian land carnivore that has ever lived, and the biggest meat-eater to live in North America since the Tyrannosaurous rex.

GIANT GROUND SLOTH

These iconic beasts lived throughout North and South America during the Pleistocene. Some grew to be the size of African Elephants. These giant beasts spent all day eating large amounts of vegetation.

GIANT VAMPIRE BAT

This flying creature was the largest Vampire Bat to have ever lived. During the Pleistocene, these large bats fed on the blood of South American mega-beasts like the Giant Sloth.

GIGANTOPITHECUS

Gigantopithecus was the largest ape to have ever existed, growing to 10 feet tall and more than 1,000 pounds. Living in Asia, this big ape had a diet similar to the Panda Bear, eating tough plants like bamboo.

IRISH ELK

Perhaps the name "Giant Deer" is more appropriate for this beast as it is more closely related to deer than to elk. This large deer had antlers 12 feet across that weighed up to 90 pounds each.

LONG-HORNED BISON

Eight feet tall at the shoulder and weighing 4,500 pounds, this was the largest bison species to have ever lived. It is especially known for its long horns, which measured nearly 8 feet across.

MACRAUCHENIA

This South American herbivore is identified by its strange looking trunk nose. Thanks to sturdy leg joints, this animal could run fast and change directions quickly. This helped it to outrun predators like Saber-toothed Cats.

MARSUPIAL LION

Related to the Kola Bear, the Marsupial Lion had one of the strongest bites of any mammal, living or extinct. The size of a small lion, this marsupial may have dropped on prey from trees, earning the nickname, "Drop Bear".

MASTODON

Often mistaken for the Woolly Mammoth, the Mastodon was quite different. This large elephant had long, upward curving tusks and, unlike Mammoths who grazed on low grasses, fed by browsing on forest trees.

MEGALANIA

Megalania is closely related to the extant Komodo Dragon, but was much, much larger. Reaching lengths of 15 to 20 feet, this Australian beast was the largest land-living lizard of all time.

MEGALODON

Megalodon was the largest shark to have ever existed, and was one of the most powerful predators ever. Before going extinct at the beginning of the Pleistocene, this 60-foot shark was an active predator of large whales.

MEIOLANIA

This large Australian turtle was distinguished by the horns on its head and big spiky tail, both uncommon traits among turtles. Meiolania did not go extinct until about 2,000 years ago, most likely due to human hunting.

MOUSE GOAT

At around one and a half feet tall, this creature was neither a mouse nor a goat. It was more closely related to sheep. Its tiny size is due to the fact that these creatures lived only on a few small islands near Spain where there were no large predators.

SABERTOOTH SALMON

At nine feet long, this strange fish had two fangs protruding from the sides of its face. These unique tusks may have been used for defense, interspecies fights, or even as a means for the fish to identify their own kind.

SCIMITAR CAT

Unlike other cats, the Scimitar Cat was built for long distance running, similar to a hyena or a wolf. It could run down prey and then dispatch it with its long, slashing teeth.

SHORT-FACED KANGAROO

This was the biggest kangaroo to have ever existed, growing up to 6 and a half feet tall and weighing up to 500 pounds. The Short-Faced Kangaroo had one large claw on each foot and didn't hop like its modern relatives, but rather walked upright in a fashion similar to a human.

SIVATHERIUM

This odd-looking beast was closely related to the modern giraffe. However, Sivatherium's neck, unlike its modern counterpart, was packed with dense muscles to support the large antlers on its head. The antlers were likely used both to shake food loose from bushes as well as for combat.

SMILODON

This Saber-toothed Cat used its heavy build and strong limbs to wrestle prey to the ground and its famous teeth to deliver a quick killing bite. Each saber tooth was over 11 inches long.

STAG MOOSE

The Stag Moose was a large North American deer. Each antler was around 6 feet long and, like living species of deer, was used for fighting, defense, and to attract mates.

STEGODON

At first glance, Stegodon looks like a modern elephant. However, unlike other elephants, Stegodon's 10 foot tusks stuck straight out and were so close together that the animal's trunk probably draped to the side as opposed to between the tusks.

TERROR BIRD

Eight feet tall and more than 300 pounds, the Terror Bird was a powerful predator. Though flightless, this bird could run very fast. It used a huge, hook-like beak to kill large prey such as this prehistoric rodent.

TOXODON

At 3,500 pounds, the massive Toxodon used its size to deter predators while it grazed on vast South American grasslands. Eventually, Toxodon was heavily hunted by humans, contributing to its extinction.

WOOLLY MAMMOTH

Perhaps the most famous Ice Age beast, the Woolly Mammoth is known for its large size, long curving tusks, and thick fur. The mammoth was perfectly adapted to life in the Ice Age. Able to defend themselves from most predators, Woolly Mammoths were ultimately extensively hunted by humans.

WOOLLY RHINOCEROS

This giant rhino could grow to weigh up to 6,000 pounds. Covered in heavy fur, the Woolly Rhino lived on the grasslands of Europe and Asia. The large horns were used for attracting mates as well as fighting and defense.